Sam and the others were playing football w
"He's one of the by-pass men!" said Sam. "l
up to."
They all ran over to the man.

"What are you up to?" asked Sam.
The man smiled. It was not a nice smile.
"There is going to be another by-pass meeting," he said. "I'll show the Council what a mess this hill is. Then they *will* build the by-pass here. You won't stop me this time!"

What are you up to?

Sam ran into the Post Office to tell Mum and Grandad.
"I knew it," said Mum. "I knew they'd try again. We can't stop the by-pass forever."
"You're right," said Grandad. "Who can help us this time?"
Just then Sam saw a poster on the wall.

Sam smiled a big smile.

"Big Money Max can!" he said. "He likes to help people."

Big Money Max had lots and lots of money. He was going to give some of it to the town.

Hops Hill Competition!
Ideas wanted for Hops Hill!
Big money for the best idea!

Big Money Max

"We can go in for the competition," said Sam. "If we win, the Council will let us build *our* idea and they won't build the by-pass. The Council won't say no to Big Money Max."

"That's a very good idea, Sam," said Grandad. "I'll go straight to the town hall. I'll find out more about the competition."
"Cool!" said Sam.

Cool!

Grandad was smiling when he got home.
"You were right, Sam," he said at tea-time. "The Council said that if we win the competition, they won't build the by-pass here."
"But what can we do with the hill?" said Mum.
"Lots of things," Sam said. "Let's call a meeting!"

"You were right, Sam.

Sam's meeting was the next day. All the boys and girls came.
"Right!" said Sam. "I want lots of ideas for the hill. Put your hand up if you have a good idea."
Lots of hands shot up.

Everyone shouted out their ideas.
Ravi had to write them down.
Lots of ideas were very good, but some were *not* so good.

Sam and Ravi took the ideas to Grandad.
They looked at all of them.
They kept all the good ideas. They threw away all the ones that were *not* so good. The very best idea was to build a park.
"Now I think we need a meeting for the grown-ups," said Grandad.

Sam and Ravi made posters about the next meeting. They put up the posters all over town.

The meeting was in the school hall. Lots and lots of grown-ups were there. Grandad told everyone about the idea to build a park.
"Put up your hand if you like the idea!" said Grandad.
All the hands shot up.

Kim's dad got up. Kim's dad was a builder.
"If we win, my men will build the park," he said.
"Hurray!" shouted everyone.
Then Ravi's dad got up. He worked with computers.
"I'll draw the plans for it on my computer," said Ravi's dad.
"Hurray!" shouted everyone.

"Hurray!"

"Hurray!"

"There is just one snag," said Grandad. "The snag is, if we win, we will still need lots of money to build our park. The competition will only give us some of the money."
"How can we get lots of money?" said Sam.
"A quiz!" shouted Sam's dad.
"And a bingo night!" said Mrs Cherry.
"And a dance!" said Kim.
Grandad and Sam smiled.

Everyone helped.
First of all they had a quiz. Everyone came.
Then they had a bingo night. Lots of money came in.

Then they had a big dance in the school hall. Everyone came. Some people could dance well – and some people could not. Lots of money came in.

Sam did a sponsored bike ride on Info-rider. He went miles and miles. Everyone sponsored him. Lots and lots of money came in!

Next they had a fair. It was a very big fair. There were stalls all along the street. There were cake stalls, sweet stalls, plant stalls and toy stalls. Lots of money came in.

Then there were games on the hill. There were games for everyone. Everyone came. Even more money came in.

Last of all was a big parade.
It went all along the streets of Hops Hill. Kim was the queen of the parade. Sam and Ravi helped to get the money.

Soon it was all over. Everyone went back to the school hall.
"How much money did we get altogether?" said Sam.
"Let's count it and see!" said Grandad.
It took a long time to count all the money.

When all the money had been counted, Grandad stood up. "Altogether we have got… three thousand pounds!" he said.
"Hurray!" shouted everyone. "Hurray! Hurray!"
"Let's hope we win the competition now," said Sam. "Let's hope we win!" He crossed his fingers.

Two days later, a letter came.
Sam crossed his fingers and screwed up his eyes.
Mum crossed her fingers and screwed up her eyes.
Grandad opened the letter.

"We've won!" yelled Grandad. "We've won!"
"Yes!" yelled Sam. "No more by-pass ever!"
"And our very own park, too," said Mum. "Our very own park."

"We've won!"